811
A

Angelou

Just give me a cool drink of
water 'fore I diiie.

By Maya Angelou

I Know Why the Caged Bird Sings

*Just Give Me a Cool Drink
of Water 'fore I Diiie*

Just Give Me
a Cool Drink
of Water
'fore I Diiie

RANDOM HOUSE 🏠 NEW YORK

Just Give Me a Cool Drink of Water 'fore I Diiie

THE POETRY OF

Maya Angelou

ISBN: 0-394-47142-3

Library of Congress Catalog Card Number: 70-156964

Manufactured in the United States of America
By The Book Press, Brattleboro, Vermont
Designed by Andrew Roberts

9 8 7 6 5 4 3

To AMBER SAM

and the ZORRO MAN

CONTENTS

PART ONE

Where Love Is a Scream of Anguish

They Went Home   3

The Gamut   4

A Zorro Man   5

To a Man   6

Late October   7

No Loser, No Weeper   8

When You Come to Me   9

Remembering   10

In a Time   11

Tears   12

The Detached   13

To a Husband   14

Accident   15

Let's Majeste   16

After   17

The Mothering Blackness   18

On Diverse Deviations   19

Mourning Grace   20

How I Can Lie to You   21

Sounds Like Pearls   22

PART TWO

Just Before the World Ends

When I Think About Myself   25

On a Bright Day, Next Week   26

Letter to an Aspiring Junkie   27

Miss Scarlett, Mr. Rhett
and Other Latter-Day Saints   28

Times-Square-Shoeshine-Composition   30

Faces   32

To a Freedom Fighter   33

Riot: 60's   34

We Saw Beyond Our Seeming   36

Black Ode   37

No No No No   38

My Guilt   42

The Calling of Names   43

On Working White Liberals   44

Sepia Fashion Show   45

The Thirteens (Black)   46

The Thirteens (White)   47

Harlem Hopscotch   48

PART ONE

Where Love Is a Scream of Anguish

A Zorro Man

Here
in the wombed room
silk purple drapes
flash a light as subtle
as your hands before
love-making

Here
in the covered lens
I catch a
clitoral image of
your general inhabitation
long and like a
late dawn in winter

Here
this clean mirror
traps me unwilling
in a gone time
when I was love
and you were booted and brave
and trembling for me.

To a Man

My man is
Black Golden Amber
Changing.
Warm mouths of Brandy Fine
Cautious sunlight on a patterned rug
Coughing laughter, rocked on a whorl of French tobacco
Graceful turns on woolen stilts
Secretive?
A cat's eye.
Southern. Plump and tender with navy bean sullenness
And did I say "Tender"?
The gentleness
A big cat stalks through stubborn bush
And did I mention "Amber"?
The heatless fire consuming itself.
Again. Anew. Into ever neverlessness.
My man is Amber
Changing
Always into itself
New. Now New.
Still itself.
Still.

Late October

Carefully
the leaves of autumn
sprinkle down the tinny
sound of little dyings
and skies sated
of ruddy sunsets
of roseate dawns
roil ceaselessly in
cobweb greys and turn
to black
for comfort.

Only lovers
see the fall
a signal end to endings
a gruffish gesture alerting
those who will not be alarmed
that we begin to stop
in order simply
to begin
again.

No Loser, No Weeper

"I hate to lose something,"
    then she bent her head
"even a dime, I wish I was dead.
I can't explain it. No more to be said.
Cept I hate to lose something."

"I lost a doll once and cried for a week.
She could open her eyes, and do all but speak.
I believe she was took, by some doll-snatching-sneak
I tell you, I hate to lose something."

"A watch of mine once, got up and walked away.
It had twelve numbers on it and for the time of day.
I'll never forget it and all I can say
Is I really hate to lose something."

"Now if I felt that way bout a watch and a toy,
What you think I feel bout my lover-boy?
I ain't threatening you madam, but he is my evening's joy.
And I mean I really hate to lose something."

When You Come to Me

When you come to me, unbidden,
Beckoning me
    To long-ago rooms,
Where memories lie.

Offering me, as to a child, an attic,
Gatherings of days too few.
    Baubles of stolen kisses.
Trinkets of borrowed loves.
    Trunks of secret words,

I CRY.

Remembering

Soft grey ghosts crawl up my sleeve
to peer into my eyes
while I within deny their threats
and answer them with lies.

Mushlike memories perform
a ritual on my lips
I lie in stolid hopelessness
and they lay my soul in strips.

In a Time

In a time of secret wooing
Today prepares tomorrow's ruin
Left knows not what right is doing
My heart is torn asunder.

In a time of furtive sighs
Sweet hellos and sad goodbyes
Half-truths told and entire lies
My conscience echoes thunder

In a time when kingdoms come
Joy is brief as summer's fun
Happiness, its race has run
Then pain stalks in to plunder.

Tears

Tears
The crystal rags
Viscous tatters
of a worn-through soul

Moans
Deep swan song
Blue farewell
of a dying dream.

The Detached

We die,
Welcoming Bluebeards to our darkening closets,
Stranglers to our outstretched necks.
      Stranglers, who neither care nor
      care to know that
      DEATH IS INTERNAL.

We pray,
Savoring sweet the teethed lies,
Bellying the grounds before alien gods
      Gods, who neither know nor
      wish to know that
      HELL IS INTERNAL.

We love,
Rubbing the nakednesses with gloved hands
Inverting our mouths in tongued kisses,
      Kisses that neither touch nor
      care to touch if
      LOVE IS INTERNAL.

To a Husband

Your voice at times a fist
      Tight in your throat
Jabs ceaselessly at phantoms
      In the room,
Your hand a carved and
      skimming boat
Goes down the Nile
      To point out Pharoah's tomb.

You're Africa to me
      At brightest dawn.
The Congo's green and
      Copper's brackish hue,
A continent to build
      With Black Man's brawn.
I sit at home and see it all
      Through you.

Accident

tonight
    when you spread your pallet
of magic,
    I escaped.
sitting apart,
    I saw you grim and unkempt.
Your vulgar-ness
    not of living
your demands
    not from need.

tonight
    as you sprinkled your brain-dust
of rainbows,
    I had no eyes.
Seeing all
I saw the colors fade
and change.
    The blood, red dulled
through the dyes,
and the naked
Black-White truth.

Let's Majeste

I sit a throne upon the times
when Kings are rare and
Consorts
slide into the grease of scullery maids.

So gaily wave a crown of light
(astride the royal chair) that blinds
the commoners who genuflect and cross their fingers.

The years will lie beside me
on the queenly bed.
And coupled we'll await
the ages' dust to cake my lids again.

And when the rousing kiss is given,
why must it always be a fairy, and
only just a Prince?

After

No sound falls
from the moaning sky
No scowl wrinkles
the evening pool
    The stars lean down
    A stony brilliance
    While birds fly

The market leers
its empty shelves
Streets bare bosoms
to scanty cars
    This bed yawns
    beneath the weight
    of our absent selves.

The Mothering Blackness

She came home running
    back to the mothering blackness
    deep in the smothering blackness
white tears icicle gold plains of her face
    She came home running

She came down creeping
    here to the black arms waiting
    now to the warm heart waiting
rime of alien dreams befrost her rich brown face
    She came down creeping

She came home blameless
    black yet as Hagar's daughter
    tall as was Sheba's daughter
threats of northern winds die on the desert's face
    She came home blameless

On Diverse Deviations

When love is a shimmering curtain
Before a door of chance
That leads to a world in question
Wherein the macabrous dance
Of bones that rattle in silence
Of blinded eyes and rolls
Of thick lips thin, denying
A thousand powdered moles,
Where touch to touch is feel
And life a weary whore
      I would be carried off, not gently
      To a shore,
      Where love is the scream of anguish
      And no curtain drapes the door.

Mourning Grace

If today, I follow death
go down its trackless wastes,
salt my tongue on hardened tears
for my precious dear times waste
race
along that promised cave in a headlong
deadlong
haste,
Will you
have
the
grace
to mourn for
me?

How I Can Lie to You

now thread my voice
with lies
of lightness
force within
my mirror eyes
the cold disguise
of sad and wise
decisions.

Sounds Like Pearls

Sounds
> Like pearls
Roll off your tongue
> To grace this eager ebon ear.

Doubt and fear,
> Ungainly things,
With blushings
> Disappear.

PART TWO

Just Before
the World Ends

When I Think About Myself

When I think about myself,
I almost laugh myself to death,
My life has been one great big joke,
A dance that's walked
A song that's spoke,
I laugh so hard I almost choke
When I think about myself.

Sixty years in these folks' world
The child I works for calls me girl
I say "Yes ma'am" for working's sake.
Too proud to bend
Too poor to break,
I laugh until my stomach ache,
When I think about myself.

My folks can make me split my side,
I laughed so hard I nearly died,
The tales they tell, sound just like lying,
They grow the fruit,
But eat the rind,
I laugh until I start to crying,
When I think about my folks.

On a Bright Day, Next Week

On a bright day, next week
Just before the bomb falls
Just before the world ends,
   Just before I die

All my tears will powder
Black in dust like ashes
Black like Buddha's belly
   Black and hot and dry

Then will mercy tumble
Falling down in godheads
Falling on the children
   Falling from the sky

Letter to an Aspiring Junkie

Let me hip you to the streets,
Jim,
Ain't nothing happening.
Maybe some tomorrows gone up in smoke,
raggedy preachers, telling a joke
to lonely, son-less old ladies' maids.

Nothing happening,
Nothing shakin', Jim.
A slough of young cats riding that
cold, white horse,
a grey old monkey on their back, of course
does rodeo tricks.

No haps, man.
No haps.
A worn-out pimp, with a space-age conk,
setting up some fool for a game of tonk,
or poker or
get 'em dead and alive.

The streets?
Climb into the streets man, like you climb
into the ass end of a lion.
Then it's fine.
It's a bug-a-loo and a shing-a-ling,
African dreams on a buck-and-a-wing and a prayer.
That's the streets man,
Nothing happening.

Miss Scarlett, Mr. Rhett
and Other Latter-Day Saints

Novitiates sing Ave
Before the whipping posts,
Criss-crossing their breasts and
tear-stained robes
in the yielding dark.

Animated by the human sacrifice
(Golgotha in black-face)
Priests glow purely white on the
bar-relief of a plantation shrine.

(O Sing)
You are gone but not forgotten
Hail, Scarlett. Requiescat in pace.

God-Makers smear brushes in
blood/gall
to etch frescoes on your
ceilinged tomb.

(O Sing)
Hosanna, King Kotton.

Shadowed couplings of infidels
tempt stigmata from the nipples
of your true-believers.

(Chant Maternoster)
Hallowed Little Eva.

Ministers make novena with the
charred bones of four
very small
very black
very young children

(Intone D I X I E)

And guard the relics
of your intact hymen
daily putting to death,
into eternity,
The stud, his seed,
His seed
His seed.

(O Sing)
Hallelujah, pure Scarlett
Blessed Rhett, the Martyr.

Times-Square-Shoeshine-Composition

I'm the best that ever done it
(pow pow)
    that's my title and I won it
    (pow pow)
I ain't lying, I'm the best
(pow pow)
    Come and put me to the test
    (pow pow)

I'll clean 'em til they squeak
(pow pow)
    In the middle of next week,
    (pow pow)
I'll shine 'em til they whine
(pow pow)
    Till they call me master mine
    (pow pow)

For a quarter and a dime
(pow pow)
    You can get the dee luxe shine
    (pow pow)
Say you wanta pay a quarter?
(pow pow)
    Then you give that to your daughter
    (pow pow)

I ain't playing dozens mister
(pow pow)
　　You can give it to your sister
　　(pow pow)
Any way you want to read it
(pow pow)
　　Maybe it's your momma need it.
　　(pow pow)

Say I'm like a greedy bigot,
(pow pow)
　　I'm a cap'tilist, can you dig it?
　　(pow pow)

Faces

Faces and more remember
then reject
the brown caramel days of youth
Reject the sun-sucked tit of
childhood mornings.
Poke a muzzle of war in the trust frozen eyes
                                 of a favored doll
Breathe, Brother
and displace a moment's hate with organized love.
A poet screams "CHRIST WAITS AT THE SUBWAY!"
But who sees?

To a Freedom Fighter

You drink a bitter draught.
I sip the tears your eyes fight to hold
A cup of lees, of henbane steeped in chaff.
Your breast is hot,
Your anger black and cold,
Through evening's rest, you dream
I hear the moans, you die a thousands' death.
When cane straps flog the body
dark and lean, you feel the blow,
I hear it in your breath.

Riot: 60's

Our
YOUR FRIEND CHARLIE pawnshop
was a glorious blaze
I heard the flames lick
then eat the trays
of zircons
mounted in red gold alloys

Easter clothes and stolen furs
burned in the attic
radios and teevees
crackled with static
plugged in
only to a racial outlet

Some
thought the FRIENDLY FINANCE FURNITURE CO.
burned higher
When a leopard print sofa with gold legs
(which makes into a bed)
caught fire
an admiring groan from the waiting horde
"Absentee landlord
you got that shit"

Lighting: a hundred Watts
Detroit, Newark and New York
Screeching nerves, exploding minds
lives tied to
a policeman's whistle
a welfare worker's doorbell
finger.

Hospitality, southern-style
corn pone grits and you-all smile
whole blocks novae
brand new stars
policemen caught in their
brand new cars
Chugga chugga chigga
git me one nigga
lootin' n burnin'
he wont git far

Watermelons, summer ripe
grey neck bones and boiling tripe
supermarket roastin like the
noon-day sun
national guard nervous with his shiny gun
goose the motor quicker
here's my nigga picka
shoot him in the belly
shoot him while he run.

We Saw Beyond Our Seeming

We saw beyond our seeming
    These days of bloodied screaming

Of children dying bloated
    Out where the lilies floated

Of men all noosed and dangling
    Within the temples strangling

Our guilt   grey fungus growing
    We knew and lied our knowing

Deafened and unwilling
    We aided in the killing

And now our souls lie broken
    Dry tablets without token.

Black Ode

Your beauty is a thunder
and I am set a wandering—a wandering
Deafened
Down twilight tin-can alleys
And moist sounds
"OOo wee Baby, Look what you could get if your name
                                        was Willie"
Oh, to dip your words like snuff.

A laughter, black and streaming
And I am come a being—a being
Rounded
Up Baptist, aisles, so moaning
And moist sounds
"Bless her heart. Take your bed and walk.
                              You been heavy burdened"
Oh, to lick your love like tears.

No No No No

No
the two legg'd beasts
that walk like men
play stink finger in their crusty asses
while crackling babies
in napalm coats
stretch mouths to receive
burning tears
on splitting tongues
JUST GIVE ME A COOL DRINK OF WATER 'FORE I DIIIE

No
the gap legg'd whore
of the eastern shore
enticing Europe to COME
in her
and turns her pigeon shit back to me
to me
Who stoked the coal that drove the ships
which brought her over the sinuous cemetery
Of my many brothers

No
the cocktailed after noons
of what can I do.
In my white layed pink world
I've let your men cram my mouth
with their black throbbing hate
and I swallowed after
I've let your mammies
steal from my kitchens
(I was always half-amused)
I've chuckled the chins of
your topsy-haired pickaninnies.
What more can I do?
I'll never be black like you.
(HALLELUJAH)

No
the red-shoed priests riding
palanquined
in barefoot children country.
the plastered saints gazing down
beneficently
on kneeling mothers
picking undigested beans
from yesterday's shit.

(39

I have waited
toes curled, hat rolled
heart and genitals
in hand
on the back porches
of forever
in the kitchens and fields
of rejections
on the cold marble steps
of America's White Out-House
in the drop seats of buses
and the open flies of war

No more
the dream that you
will cease haunting me
down in fetid swamps of fear
and will turn to embrace your own
humanity
which I AM

No more
The hope that
the razored insults
which mercury slide over your tongue
will be forgotten
and you will learn the words of love
Mother Brother Father Sister Lover Friend

My hopes
dying slowly
rose petals falling
beneath an autumn red moon
will not adorn your unmarked graves

My dreams
lying quietly
a dark pool under the trees
will not carry your name
to a forgetful shore
And what a pity

What a pity
That pity has folded in upon itself
an old man's mouth
whose teeth are gone
and I have no pity.

My Guilt

My guilt is "slavery's chains," too long
the clang of iron falls down the years.
This brother's sold. This sister's gone
is bitter wax, lining my ears.
My guilt made music with the tears.

My crime is "heroes, dead and gone"
dead Vesey, Turner, Gabriel,
dead Malcolm, Marcus, Martin King.
They fought too hard, they loved too well.
My crime is I'm alive to tell.

My sin is "hanging from a tree"
I do not scream, it makes me proud.
I take to dying like a man.
I do it to impress the crowd.
My sin lies in not screaming loud.

The Calling of Names

He went to being called a Colored man
after answering to "hey nigger,"
Now that's a big jump,
anyway you figger,
            Hey, Baby, Watch my smoke.
From colored man to Negro
With the N in caps,
was like saying Japanese
instead of saying Japs.
            I mean, during the war.
The next big step
was a change for true,
From Negro in caps
to being a Jew.
            Now, Sing Yiddish Mama.
Light, Yellow, Brown
and Dark brown skin,
were o.k. colors to
describe him then,
            He was a Bouquet of Roses.
He changed his seasons
like an almanac,
Now you'll get hurt
if you don't call him "Black."
            Nigguh, I ain't playin' this time.

On Working White Liberals

I don't ask the Foreign Legion
Or anyone to win my freedom
Or to fight my battle better than I can,

Though there's one thing that I cry for
I believe enough to die for
That is every man's responsibility to man.

I'm afraid they'll have to prove first
that they'll watch the Black man move first
Then follow him with faith to kingdom come,
This rocky road is not paved for us,
So, I'll believe in Liberal's aid for us
When I see a white man load a Black man's gun.

Sepia Fashion Show

Their hair, pomaded, faces jaded
bones protruding, hip-wise,
The models strutted, backed and butted,
Then stuck their mouths out, lip-wise.

They'd nasty manners, held like banners,
while they looked down their nose-wise,
I'd see 'em in hell, before they'd sell
me one thing they're wearing, clothes-wise.

The Black Bourgeois, who all say "yah"
When yeah is what they're meaning
Should look around, both up and down
before they set out preening.

"Indeed" they swear, "that's what I'll wear
When I go country-clubbing,"
I'd remind them please, look at those knees
you got a Miss Ann's scrubbing.

The Thirteens (Black)

Your Momma took to shouting
Your Poppa's gone to war,
Your sister's in the streets
Your brother's in the bar,
The thirteens. Right On.

Your cousin's taking smack
Your Uncle's in the joint,
Your buddy's in the gutter
Shooting for his point
The thirteens. Right on.

And you, you make me sorry
You out here by yourself,
I'd call you something dirty,
But there just ain't nothing left,
cept
The thirteens. Right On.

The Thirteens (White)

Your Momma kissed the chauffeur,
Your Poppa balled the cook,
Your sister did the dirty,
in the middle of the book,
The thirteens. Right On.

Your daughter wears a jock strap,
Your son he wears a bra
Your brother jonesed your cousin
in the back seat of the car.
The thirteens. Right On.

Your money thinks you're something
But if I'd learned to curse,
I'd tell you what your name is
But there just ain't nothing worse
than
The thirteens. Right On.

Harlem Hopscotch

One foot down, then hop! It's hot.
    Good things for the ones that's got.
Another jump, now to the left.
    Everybody for hisself.

In the air, now both feet down.
    Since you black, don't stick around.
Food is gone, the rent is due,
    Curse and cry and then jump two.

All the people out of work,
    Hold for three, then twist and jerk.
Cross the line, they count you out.
    That's what hopping's all about.

Both feet flat, the game is done.
They think I lost. I think I won.

About the Author

During the busy years following the childhood described in her first book, *I Know Why the Caged Bird Sings*, MAYA ANGELOU studied dance in San Francisco, and toured Europe and Africa for the State Department in *Porgy and Bess*. She taught dance in Rome and Tel Aviv. In collaboration with Godfrey Cambridge, she produced, directed and starred in *Cabaret for Freedom* at New York's Village Gate; she also starred in Genet's *The Blacks* at the St. Mark's Playhouse. At the request of the late Dr. Martin Luther King, Jr., Miss Angelou became the Northern Coordinator for the Southern Christian Leadership Conference. From this she went to Africa, writing for newspapers in Cairo and Ghana, where she was on the faculty of the University of Ghana. She has written and produced a ten-part TV series on African traditions in American life. She now lives in California.